D0604119

THE CONQUISTADORS

BY JIM OLLHOFF

VISIT US AT
WWW.ABDOPUBLISHING.COM

Published by ABDO Publishing Company, 8000 West 78th Street, Suite 310, Edina, MN 55439. Copyright ©2012 by Abdo Consulting Group, Inc. International copyrights reserved in all countries. No part of this book may be reproduced in any form without written permission from the publisher. ABDO & Daughters™ is a trademark and logo of ABDO Publishing Company.

Printed in the United States of America, North Mankato, Minnesota.
052011
092011

 PRINTED ON RECYCLED PAPER

Editor: John Hamilton
Graphic Design: Sue Hamilton
Cover Design: Neil Klinepier
Cover Photo: Getty Images
Interior Photos and Illustrations: Alamy-pgs 14, 15, 17, 26 & 27; AP-pg 19; Corbis-pgs 9, 24 & 25; Getty Images-pgs 4, 5, 7, 10, 11, 12 & 13; Glow Images-pgs 21 & 28; Granger Collection-pgs 6, 22, 23 & 29; and ThinkStock-pg 8.

Library of Congress Cataloging-in-Publication Data

Ollhoff, Jim, 1959-
  The conquistadors / Jim Ollhoff.
    p. cm. -- (Hispanic American history)
  Includes index.
  ISBN 978-1-61783-055-6
  1. America--Discovery and exploration--Spanish--Juvenile literature. 2. Explorers--America--History--16th century--Juvenile literature. 3. Spain--Colonies--America--Juvenile literature. 4. Indians--First contact with Europeans--Juvenile literature. 5. Indians, Treatment of--America--Juvenile literature. I. Title. II. Series: Hispanic American history (Edina, Minn.)
  E123.O453 2012
  970.016--dc22
                        2011018112

CONTENTS

What is a Conquistador? 4

The Discovery of the Americas 8

Hernán Cortéz: Conquering the Aztecs 12

Vasco Núñez de Balboa: Seeing the Pacific Ocean 14

Francisco Pizarro: Conquering the Inca 16

Juan Ponce de León: Claiming Florida for Spain............................ 18

Juan Rodríguez Cabrillo: Up the Coast of California.............................. 20

Hernando de Soto: Exploring the Southeastern United States 22

Francisco Vásquez de Coronado: Exploring the Southwest 24

Bartolomé de Las Casas.. 26

Legacy of the Conquistadors.. 28

Glossary.. 30

Index 32

WHAT IS A CONQUISTADOR?

A conquistador was a Spanish military leader of the 16th century. These men were adventurers, explorers, and most of all, conquerors. The word conquistador means "conqueror." Conquistadors brought large areas of North and South America under Spanish control.

A few conquistadors were funded by the Spanish government, but most used their own money. They hoped that their expeditions might find gold or silver. If they came back with treasures, they knew the Spanish government would handsomely reward them.

The conquistadors were ordered to explore the new lands, look for gold, and convert Indian tribes to Christianity. Their motto was "God, glory, and gold." Often, the conquistadors were very cruel, killing the Indians and claiming their land for the Spanish crown.

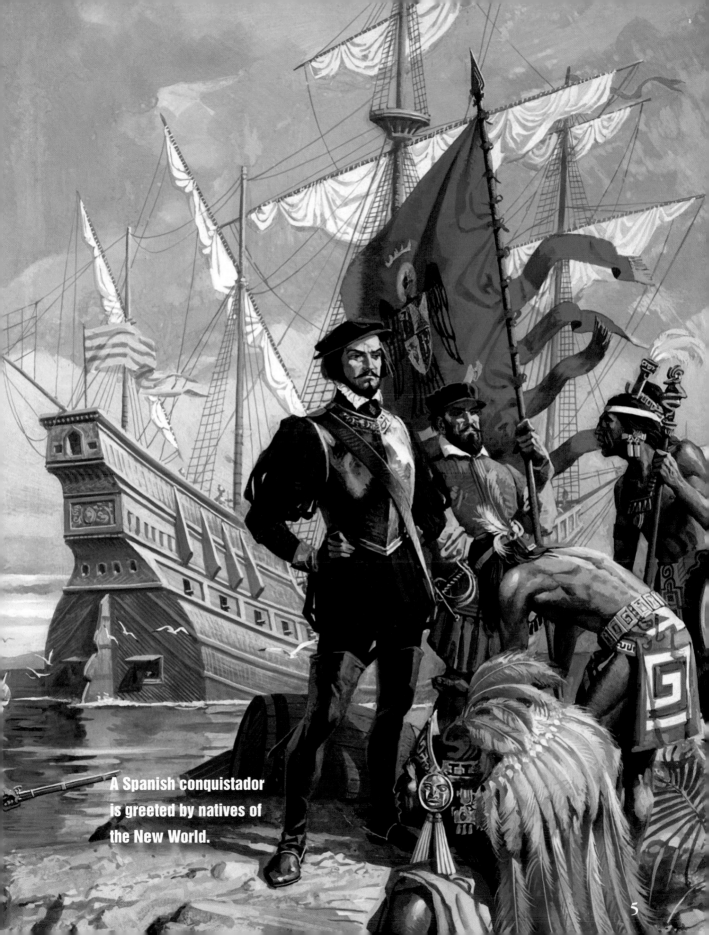

A Spanish conquistador is greeted by natives of the New World.

The conquistadors defeated much larger armies of American Indian tribes, including well-organized armies such as the Aztecs and Inca. How were they so successful? There were three main reasons.

The first reason that the conquistadors were so successful is that they were excellent politicians. When they found two kingdoms at war, they sometimes lent their military might to one side. The Aztecs, for example, had many Indian enemies. The conquistadors were able to convince thousands of Indian warriors to fight the Aztecs.

Another reason that the conquistadors were so successful is that their military technology was more advanced than that of the Indians. They had horses, which they introduced to the Americas. The Indians had never seen horses before, and the Spanish were good at using horses in battle.

The Spanish also used steel for their swords and other weapons. Steel was much harder and lasted much longer than the metals used by the Indians. The Spanish also brought firearms, which were devastating on the battlefield.

But the biggest reason for the conquistadors's success was not even planned. The Spanish unknowingly brought germs with them. They brought diseases, such as smallpox, to which the Indians had no immunity. The Indians contracted smallpox, and it spread like wildfire through their communities. It spread through Indian trade routes, infecting one community after another. In some places, 50 percent of the native Indians were killed by smallpox. In other places, 95 percent of the native Indians died. Villages were often devastated by disease before the Spanish even arrived.

Aztecs dying of smallpox.

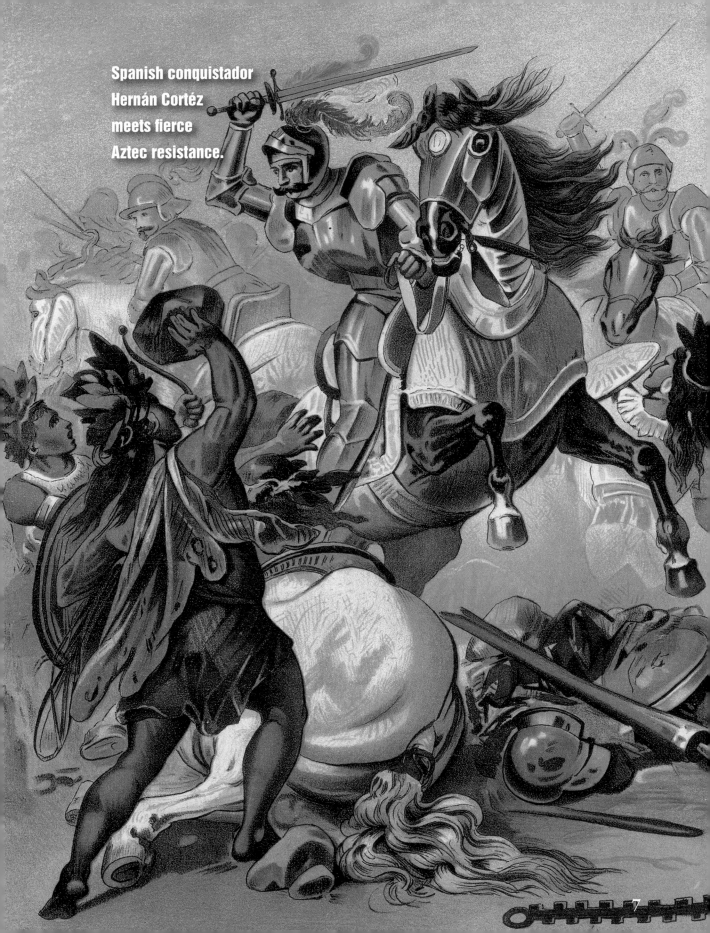

Spanish conquistador
Hernán Cortéz
meets fierce
Aztec resistance.

THE DISCOVERY OF THE AMERICAS

Columbus

In the 1400s, Western Europe wanted to trade with India and China. Asia had spices, silk, and other exotic goods. The problem was, how to get there? The trip overland was long and dangerous, a desert journey filled with bandits and wild animals. The other possibility was to sail south around Africa, and then go eastward to Asia. However, the sea trip was also very risky. The heat of the equator and violent storms made the trip dangerous. Many sailors got scurvy and other diseases. Pirates on the sea and armies on the shore made the trip very difficult.

Most educated people in Europe knew that the Earth was round. They believed it was possible to get to Asia by sailing west, but they thought it was too far. They didn't think that they could pack enough food and fresh water in the ships to make it to Asia. They also didn't realize that there was a continent between Asia and Europe.

Christopher Columbus convinced the Spanish monarchs that he could sail westward and arrive in Asia. The Spanish gave him three ships, the *Niña*, the *Pinta*, and the *Santa Maria*. He set sail in August 1492, and saw land in October. Although his exact landing place is still debated, most scholars believe he landed on the island of San Salvador in the Caribbean Sea. He believed he had landed in India, and so called the people of the islands "Indians."

In 1991, replicas of Christopher Columbus's three ships were built and sailed: the *Pinta*, the *Santa Maria*, and the *Niña*.

Ferdinand Magellan

It did not take long for Europe to realize that the land Columbus saw was not India, but a whole new continent. Spain and Portugal argued about which country "owned" the new world. In 1494, at the Spanish city of Tordesillas, they reached an agreement. Portugal would take the eastern edge of South America, today's country of Brazil. Spain would own the rest of South America and Central America.

Both Spain and Portugal were still anxious to find a way to Asia. In 1519, the Spanish funded an expedition by Ferdinand Magellan to find the way to Asia. Magellan left Spain in September 1519, sailing around the southernmost tip of South America. He died fighting a battle in the Philippines, but the ship continued to sail westward to Asia. It continued on, rounding Africa and sailing north to Spain. Magellan's ship arrived back in Spain in September 1522.

Spain was beginning to see that the Americas were full of natural resources and possibly gold. Spain became less interested in going to Asia, and more interested in exploring the Americas. They sent the conquistadors to explore and conquer.

In 1519, the Spanish funded an expedition by Ferdinand Magellan to find the way to Asia.

HERNÁN CORTÉZ: CONQUERING THE AZTECS

One of the most famous—and notorious—conquistadors was Hernán Cortéz.
He was born in 1485 in Spain. He had wealthy parents. As a young man, he chose to go to the New World, where he eventually became an administrator in Cuba. In 1519, when he had the chance to explore the mainland to the west, he jumped at the chance. He funded the expedition himself, finding more than 500 men to go with him to the Yucatán Peninsula (in today's southern Mexico).

Cortéz is most famous for this invasion of Aztec lands. Cortéz didn't see the Aztecs as a separate nation. He believed all the Indians of Central and South America were subjects of the Spanish crown. Therefore, Cortéz believed his mission was to convert them to Christianity and put them to work—sending gold and other natural resources back to Spain. Of course, the Aztecs didn't see it that way.

Cortéz gathered the many Indian enemies of the Aztecs. The Aztecs were already weakened with smallpox and other European diseases. With his Indian alliances, Cortéz was able to defeat the powerful Aztec nation in 1521.

Historians still debate Cortéz's character. To some, he was a ruthless and vicious invader. Others say he was simply stubborn and misguided. Cortéz died in Spain in 1547.

Cortéz and his troops fight Aztec warriors.

VASCO NÚÑEZ DE BALBOA: SEEING THE PACIFIC OCEAN

The conquistador Vasco Núñez de Balboa was born in Spain about 1475. He was the first European to see the Pacific Ocean from the New World.

Balboa came to the New World in 1500 to look for gold and precious stones. In 1511, he founded the first settlement in South America, in what is today the country of Colombia. He married the daughter of a nearby Indian chief. In 1513, together with local Indians, he set out to explore the western side of the continent. Traveling across Panama, fighting Indians all the way, he eventually stood on the shores of the Pacific Ocean. He claimed for Spain all the land that touched the Pacific Ocean. He fought more battles against local Indians, and stole their gold, before returning eastward across Panama.

Balboa's jealous rivals claimed that he had committed treason against Spain (a charge of which he was innocent). Fellow conquistador Francisco Pizarro arrested him, and he was executed in 1519.

Balboa raising his sword and claiming the Pacific Ocean for Spain in 1513.

FRANCISCO PIZARRO: CONQUERING THE INCA

Francisco Pizarro was born in Spain in the 1470s (the exact year is uncertain). He was a second cousin to Hernán Cortéz, the conqueror of the Aztecs.

Pizarro served in the 1513 expedition of Balboa to the Pacific Ocean. By 1522, explorations in western South America led to rumors of a fantastic civilization, rich in gold. Pizarro, wanting to make a name for himself, began to explore the land of South America and conquer Indian tribes. In 1524, he made his first journey to the Inca civilization.

A mosaic shows the last Inca emperor Atahuallpa meeting conquistador Francisco Pizarro in 1532.

His first attempt to conquer the Inca was unsuccessful, but he tried again. By 1532, the Inca were decimated by smallpox and weak from internal conflicts. They were too feeble to fight off the Spanish. Over the next several years, the Inca civilization collapsed.

Pizarro founded the city of Lima, and set himself up to be the governor of Peru. He remained the governor there for almost 10 years, overseeing the decline of the Inca culture. One of Pizarro's rivals assassinated him in 1541.

JUAN PONCE DE LEÓN: CLAIMING FLORIDA FOR SPAIN

The conquistador Juan Ponce de León is often credited with being the first European to land in Florida. In 1493, he joined Christopher Columbus's second voyage to the Americas. They arrived at the island of Hispaniola (today's Haiti and the Dominican Republic). He was eventually put in charge of a large province. Later, he explored the island of Puerto Rico, looking for gold and searching for places to put settlements.

In 1513, following rumors of a land to the north, Ponce de León took some ships and men and landed in Florida, which they believed at first to be another island. He named the land Florida because there were so many flowers. It was the Easter season, which the Spanish called the Festival of Flowers (*Pascua Florida*).

In 1521, he attempted to bring colonists to settle in Florida. They were attacked by a Native American tribe, and Ponce de León was wounded with a poisoned arrow. He died later from his wounds.

Some historians think Ponce de León was looking for the Fountain of Youth, a mythical body of water that was rumored to make people young again. More likely, that story was invented by his political rivals to make him appear foolish and unreliable.

18

Juan Ponce de León was struck by a poison arrow while attempting to bring Spanish colonists to Florida. He later died of his injuries.

JUAN RODRÍGUEZ CABRILLO:
UP THE COAST OF CALIFORNIA

Historians differ on whether Juan Rodríguez Cabrillo was born in Spain or Portugal. However, he ended up working for the Spanish, and even served in the army of Hernán Cortéz in the 1519 battle against the Aztecs.

Cabrillo went on other military expeditions, fighting Indian nations in Central and South America. He was rewarded with a grant of land in Guatemala, where he settled. Not one to stay in one place for long, he started a shipbuilding company.

In 1542, he sailed up the coast of California. He explored San Diego Bay, landing on the point that is now the Cabrillo National Monument. He continued north past San Francisco Bay. He explored several islands along the coast. He was hoping to find a water passage from the Atlantic Ocean to the Pacific Ocean. He also hoped to open up trade with the Spice Islands in the Pacific Ocean (in today's Indonesia). In November 1542, on Santa Catalina Island off the shore of Southern California, he was injured in a fall, and died in January 1543.

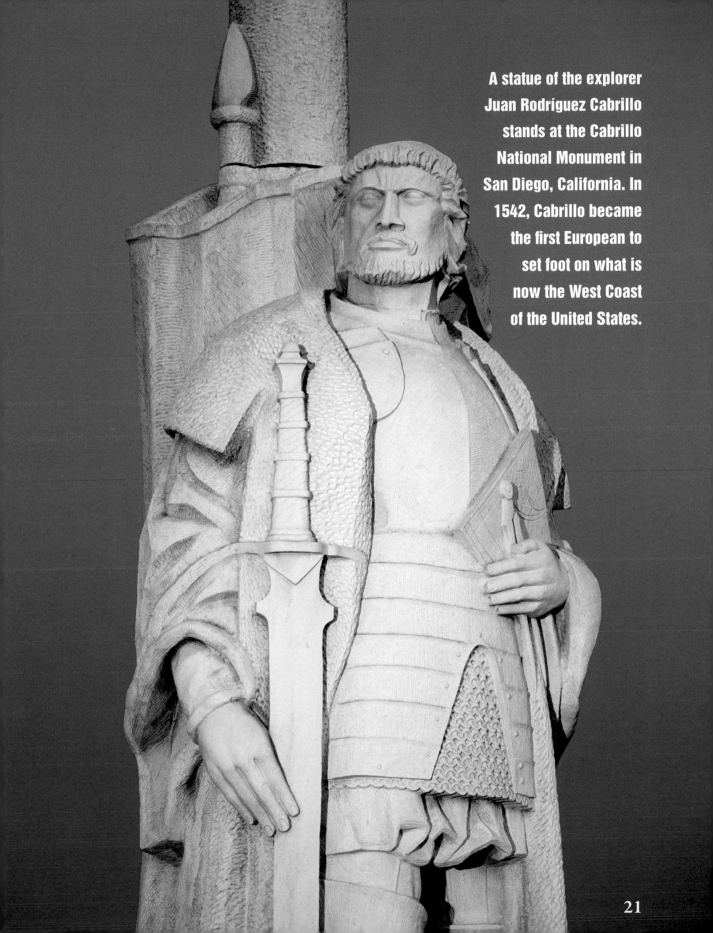

A statue of the explorer Juan Rodríguez Cabrillo stands at the Cabrillo National Monument in San Diego, California. In 1542, Cabrillo became the first European to set foot on what is now the West Coast of the United States.

HERNANDO DE SOTO: EXPLORING THE SOUTHEASTERN UNITED STATES

In 1539, Hernando de Soto landed in Florida determined to find gold and places to settle.

With little money, but a desire for adventure, Hernando de Soto came to Central America in 1514. By the 1520s, he was exploring today's Costa Rica and Honduras, looking for gold and suitable places for settlement. By 1524, he fought in battles to conquer Nicaragua. In 1531, he helped Francisco Pizarro in his quest to conquer the Inca.

The Spanish crown rewarded de Soto for his work by giving him the authority to explore, conquer, and settle in today's southeastern United States. But he had to do it at his own expense. So, in 1539, he and more than 600 men landed in Florida, determined to find gold and places to settle.

By 1540, de Soto's expedition had marched up the coast of Florida and into Georgia. Following rumors of gold and precious jewels, he traveled into today's North and South Carolina and Tennessee. By May 1541, de Soto was at the Mississippi River near today's city of Memphis, Tennessee. He crossed the Mississippi River into Arkansas, becoming probably the first European to cross the river.

About half of de Soto's men had already been killed by sickness and in battles with Indian nations. In May 1542, along the Mississippi River, de Soto also died from an illness. The rest of his men floated on rafts down the Mississippi River to the Gulf of Mexico, and then made it back to Mexico.

FRANCISCO VÁSQUEZ DE CORONADO: EXPLORING THE SOUTHWEST

Coronado searched today's southwestern United States for "cities of gold."

Francisco Vásquez de Coronado was born in Spain in 1510. He came to Mexico around 1535 and within a few years became governor of one of the Spanish provinces. However, he was more interested in gold and adventure. There were rumors about "cities of gold," and Coronado wanted to find them. In 1540, he outfitted a massive expedition, including about 300 Spanish soldiers, more than 1,000 Indians, and huge livestock herds.

Coronado explored parts of today's Arizona, New Mexico, Texas, Oklahoma, and even areas of Kansas. Some of his men found the Grand Canyon. Of course, he never found the cities of gold, which led others to think that his journey was a failure.

Coronado returned to his position as governor, but he was accused of cruelty to the Indians. He was removed from his office in 1544, and sent to a minor governmental position in Mexico City. He died in 1554.

BARTOLOMÉ DE LAS CASAS

Not all of the Spanish residents of the New World were looking for gold. There were some who were looking to create a better world, and not treat Indian nations as slaves and second-class citizens.

Bartolomé de Las Casas was not a conquistador. He was born in Spain, and he came to the island of Hispaniola (today's Haiti and the Dominican Republic) in 1502. He became a priest in 1510, and he worked tirelessly to improve conditions for the Indian people and to end Spain's cruel treatment of them.

He was able to get some laws passed that improved the treatment of the Indians, but those laws were often not enforced. The large landowners needed a lot of workers to grow crops, and since slave labor was free, the landowners profited greatly. Gradually, perhaps due to his constant advocacy in Europe and in the New World, slave labor became less common.

Bartolomé de Las Casas wrote a history of the Spanish conquest of the land, called *A History of the Devastation of the Indies*. Las Casas was perhaps the first civil rights champion in the New World. He died in Spain in 1566.

Bartolomé de Las Casas worked to protect native Indian people.

LEGACY OF THE CONQUISTADORS

A gold statue from Lima, Peru.

The conquistadors spent a huge amount of time and money looking for gold. Except for the civilizations of the Aztecs and Inca, very little gold was found.

The conquistadors were usually cruel and ruthless in their meetings with the Native Americans.

The conquistadors demanded that the Indian nations become Catholic and obey Spanish laws, and if they did not, the conquistadors promised war. And war is exactly what the conquistadors got.

However, the conquistadors cleared the path for Spanish settlements. Thousands of Spanish settlers moved to the New World. Intermarriage between Spanish and Indian groups was encouraged by Spanish policies. Today, most people in Mexico have both Spanish and Indian ancestors.

The Central and South American colonies continued to grow. The Spanish and Indian cultures mixed together, and soon they became indistinguishable.

La Malince, also known as Doña Marina, was a native woman given to Hernán Cortéz in 1519. Marina became Cortéz's interpreter. Later, she gave birth to his son. Martín was one of the first children of mixed Spanish and native ancestry.

GLOSSARY

ALLIANCE

A relationship between two or more groups of people, countries, or organizations that benefits each of the groups. For example, the Spanish conquistador Hernán Cortéz made alliances with other native tribes that allowed him to conquer the more powerful Aztecs.

ANCESTORS

The people from whom a person is directly descended. This term usually refers to people in generations prior to a person's grandparents.

ASSASSINATE

To kill an important person, usually for political reasons. For example, Francisco Pizarro, the governor of Peru, was assassinated by a rival.

AZTEC

A powerful civilization in southern Mexico, emerging in the 1300s. The Aztec civilization came to an end in 1521 at the hands of Spanish conquistadors.

CIVIL RIGHTS

The freedoms and rights that protect every person from discriminatory governments and leaders.

CONQUISTADORS

Spanish military men who explored the New World and conquered many of the Indian tribes living in the Americas.

IMMUNITY

The human immune system "remembers" when viruses or bacteria attack the body. From then on, the immune system can kill the germs quickly. Without immunity, people often die. Natives in the Americas experienced this lack of immunity against the European disease of smallpox. Many thousands of people died.

INCA

A civilization on the west side of South America. They emerged in the 1200s and were conquered by the Spanish in the 1530s.

MAYA

A civilization in Central America that existed from about 200 AD to about 900 AD.

NEW WORLD

The areas of North, Central, and South America, as well as islands near these land masses. The term was often used by European explorers.

SCURVY

A disease resulting from a lack of vitamin C in the body, often due to an insufficient amount of fruit in the diet. Symptoms include general weakness and bleeding gums.

SMALLPOX

An often-deadly disease unknowingly brought by the Spanish to the Americas. The native peoples had no immunity to smallpox, so it spread like wildfire throughout the American populations.

INDEX

A

Africa 8, 10
American Indians 6
Americas 6, 10, 18 (*See also* North America, Central America, and South America)
Arizona 25
Arkansas 23
Asia 8, 10
Atlantic Ocean 20
Aztecs 6, 13, 16, 20, 28

B

Balboa, Vasco Núñez de 14, 16
Brazil 10

C

Cabrillo, Juan Rodríguez 20
Cabrillo National Monument 20
California 20
Caribbean Sea 8
Catholic 28
Central America 10, 13, 20, 23, 28
China 8
Christianity 4, 13
Colombia 14
Columbus, Christopher 8, 10, 18
Coronado, Francisco Vásquez de 25
Cortéz, Hernán 12, 13, 16, 20
Costa Rica 23
Cuba 12

D

Dominican Republic 18, 26

E

Earth 8
Easter 18
Europe 8, 10, 26

F

Festival of Flowers 18 (*See also Pascua Florida*)
Florida 18, 23
Fountain of Youth 18

G

Georgia 23
Grand Canyon 25
Guatemala 20
Gulf of Mexico 23

H

Haiti 18, 26
Hispaniola 18, 26
History of the Devastation of the Indies, A 26
Honduras 23

I

Inca 6, 17, 23, 28
India 8, 10
Indians 4, 6, 8, 13, 14, 17, 25, 26, 28
Indonesia 20

K

Kansas 25

L

Las Casas, Bartolomé de 26
Lima, Peru 17

M

Magellan, Ferdinand 10
Memphis, TN 23
Mexico 12, 23, 25, 28
Mexico City 25
Mississippi River 23

N

Native Americans 28
New Mexico 25
New World 12, 14, 26, 28
Nicaragua 23

Niña 8
North America 4
North Carolina 23

O

Oklahoma 25

P

Pacific Ocean 14, 16, 20
Panama 14
Pascua Florida 18 (*See also* Festival of Flowers)
Peru 17
Philippines 10
Pinta 8
Pizarro, Francisco 14, 16, 17, 23
Ponce de León, Juan 18
Portugal 10, 20
Puerto Rico 18

S

San Diego Bay 20
San Francisco Bay 20
San Salvador 8
Santa Catalina Island 20
Santa Maria 8
Soto, Hernando de 23
South America 4, 10, 13, 14, 16, 17, 20, 28
South Carolina 23
Spain 10, 12, 13, 14, 16, 20, 25, 26
Spice Islands 20

T

Tennessee 23
Texas 25
Tordesillas 10

U

United States 23

Y

Yucatán Peninsula 12